FALSE POSITIVE

FALSE POSITIVE

Poems

Craig Graham

Vagabond Books
Pasadena 2016

False Positive by Craig Graham
Copyright 2016
Edited by Patti Graham

Cover photo, format and layout by Katie Graham
Frontispiece photo of Allen Ginsberg by Craig Graham
Rear cover photo by Archie Graham
All rights reserved

Published by Vagabond Books
www.vagabondbooks.com
Printed in the USA

ISBN: 1533685371
ISBN 13: 9781533685377

For Patti who saved me,
with thanks for a lifetime of inspiration,
the love of our growing family
and in memory of Charles Bukowski

"…pure and magic emotions hang on the simple clean line."`

-Charles Bukowski- **YOU GET SO ALONE AT TIMES THAT IT JUST MAKES SENSE**

"dooty is dooty…"

-Robert Louis Stevenson- **TREASURE ISLAND**

CONTENTS

Thirty seconds over Hiroshima · 1
False positive · 5
Breaking News June 5, 2014 · 8
Night racer · 10
Home of the free · 12
Morgue hero · 14
What they mean ·17
Hell on earth · 20
Book sale at Fort Mason · 24
Allen Ginsberg satori · 27
L. A. riots · 32
Joe Herwig · 36
Humbug · 37
Santa Cruz · 40
Rain · 45
Sheriff John · 47
Walking on tacks · 50
Imagine yourself · 53
Class warfare · 55
Vals · 57
October 31st · 60
Down · 63
For better or for worse · 65
Milk · 66
In two · 67
A rotting cantaloupe · 69

Thirty seconds over Hiroshima

My father, now 92 years old,
is a strong, stoic man of few words,
intolerant of bull shitters
and secretive about his past

As a stalwart Second Lieutenant,
Archie piloted B-24s and B-29s
and trained many
combat bomber pilots,
some of whom flew
to their deaths,
giving the ultimate
sacrifice for their country

This past March,
from the closet
where his proud and
immaculate uniform still hangs,
Dad brought out a worn grey box
containing a half dozen
World War 2 photos

One by one,
Dad slowly and gently
laid his photos out
on the kitchen table,
like puzzle pieces
re-connected,
the images of his fellow fliers
staring from

out of the past,
and he began quietly speaking
about his
war experience

For the first time
I learned that
seventy years ago
Dad's squadron
was mobilized with orders
to join
the American final air assault
on Japan

Poised to leave for battle,
sudden and shocking
newspaper headlines shouted
that on August 6, 1945,
the B-29 bomber Enola Gay
dropped "Little Boy,"
the first atomic bomb
on Hiroshima,
killing approximately 140,000 people,
and again, three days later,
Bockscar, the second American bomber,
dropped "Fat Man" on Nagasaki,
killing 40,000 more Japanese

Ignorant of our top commands'
closely kept secret
that we hadn't another
atomic bomb to drop-
Emperor Hirohito announced
Japan's unconditional surrender

on August 15, 1945,
ending the war in Asia and the Pacific,
canceling my father's final engagement
with our mortal enemy,
who'd sworn to fight
and die to the last man,
woman and child

This savage slaughter of our enemy,
not only likely saved my
father's life
and tens of thousands of Allied and
American soldiers
but our unborn lives as well,
my future brother and sisters
who would be gifted life
along with millions
of "baby boomers"
because these lucky bombs
of mass destruction
forced the devastating
war to end

As I stared in wonder
at the young
time frozen faces
of the men
looking brave and determined
in Dad's photos,
people I'd never met,
I saw his personal history
come alive in events
that forever changed
world history

Dad's memories,
too impossible to speak of
all these years
and the profound personal meaning
his war photos held for him,
their closely held,
long secret history,
a humble reminder
of the untold sacrifices and the
tragedy of it all
that lives on
in us

False positive

Your sudden death
came as such
a huge shock

Only the other day
we were out having
a few drinks,
laughing and joking,
celebrating
the good news
of the positive results
from your yearly physical exam

Beaming and a little cocky
you quoted your doctor who declared you
"in perfect health"

Of course you were
All your friends knew it
There was never any doubt
We admired your upbeat,
endless energy and enthusiasm,
often wondering where
you got it from

You exercised daily,
stayed fit and trim,
ate wisely and well,
never smoked,

got 8 hours of sleep
most nights,
took regular vacations,
and lucky you,
never needed glasses,
not that glasses
had anything to do with it

You were doing
everything right and
living a good life
Even your colonoscopy doctor
joked that your colon
was so clean
you could eat off of it

You loved your wife
and your kids and your work
and you had
everything to live for

I don't get it

After the autopsy
to solve the mystery
of your premature death,
after the technicians
had gutted you
and dissected your organs
and weighed and measured your brain
and sifted through your blood
and remaining parts,
the pathologist uttered,

in quiet, solemn words
meant to provide comfort
to your loved ones
about your incomprehensible
and untimely death,
to force a speck of understanding
for your lost life,
"His heart gave out…it happens."

I thought you'd want to know

Breaking News
June 5, 2014

In LA
there's a cluster of
state-of-the art
medical buildings
located around the intersection
of Vermont and Sunset,
a nexus of hospitals
offering hope
and treatment
for patients
determined to live

On the second floor
of the Kaiser Hospital radiology department,
the waiting room TV
baby-sits nervous appointees

A sudden BREAKING NEWS story
interrupts a game show
to report another "senseless"
street killing of a local gangster,
mowed down
in front of a Taco Bell next to a middle school
in trendy Silverlake

Another barely newsworthy
sound bite of entertainment,
this routine

drive by murder story
quickly vanishes from the screen

East-bound,
post-procedure
forty-five relieved minutes later,
the cops have blocked off
bustling Sunset Blvd at Fountain
with squad cars
flashing red lights
as a fresh corpse lies
roasting
on the fiery pavement

So dead, so damned finished, so wasted

Pissed off motorists,
surging like blood
in a pinched artery,
roiled by the delay,
ignorant of the crime before them,
angrily honk and scream curses and jockey
their cars to escape

By 10 p.m. the local nightly news
has already dropped the
tedious story of the street killing,
upstaged by stories of a
Hollywood Bowl fraudulent ticket scam
followed by two other
American mass murders
on the same day

Business as usual for the breaking heart news

Night racer

Black night
embraces you
with phantom
lover arms
High beams
push back
each shrieking moment
Tires squeal on asphalt
like terrified pigs
fleeing Jimmy Dean's
slaughterhouse

Tense eager hands
grip the wheel you
synchronize to the throttle,
hi-octane music
fuels every crazy
red-lined second,
a passionate function
of natural selection

You charge this worn
and practiced route
riddled with predatory cops
in the otherwise calm
dead of night
flat out,
adrenalin hooked
on excitement

19 year-old heart racing,
pipes blasting,
a single blunder
could snap your
escape
in half

Home of the free

Barbeque sizzling,
cool drinks flowing,
old friends gather
to celebrate
the birthday of America

Bruce Springsteen blasts out
"Dancing in the Dark," while
Beach Boys music
surfs over the fence
from a neighbor's back yard party,
pounding out the beats
to the larger sounds
of sweet fireworks
exploding in all directions
concussing the skies

A breaking news story
replays a citizen video of a CHP cop
beating the crap
out of a hapless
elderly black grandmother
he tackled for walking alongside
the 10 freeway in LA

As I do every 4th of July,
I safely shoot off
my fair share of fireworks,
risking a $1,000 fine by the city

I know my human rights,
I know my civil rights
Whose home of the free
and land of the brave
is this anyway?

Morgue hero

In Pico Rivera
the cops shot and killed
another innocent citizen

In their perpetual
police confusion
of good guy-bad guy,
the cops chose
to use deadly force
against the unarmed good guy,
guessing wrong
yet again,
just like the McDade police murder
in Pasadena

After The City paid off
McDade's grieving parents
"about $1 million,"
a purposely delayed
two year investigative report
into his killing
is kept secret from the public
who paid for all of it
kept SECRET-
while the police shooters
sit back, alive, safely redacted and
still on the job,
collecting their obscene paychecks

What are the police
and the city government hiding
that we have a right to know?

Where is the justice?

All across America,
why does this keep happening?
What does it take to
police the police?

The police chief of Los Angeles
is caught vehemently lying
about a seemingly crooked inside police deal
involving himself
and a family member,
betraying his sworn oath
"To protect and serve"

Despite the scandals
the chief was reappointed
for four more years

Where is the justice?

Why is it necessary
to teach children to
fear the police?
How can you tell
the good cops
from the bad ones?

When trigger-happy cops
decide in a split
second to execute
somebody,
why do they choose to murder the innocent?
Is that what the police are trained to do?
Couldn't the shooter
hold his kill shot
until they were absolutely certain
of their victim?
Are cops getting kickbacks
from the undertakers?

That's how it went down again yesterday
and today a police spokesman issued
a contrite statement,
approved, if not written,
by the city's lawyers,
while the bereaved family plans their funeral
for their dead hero,
lying in a morgue

The police "sorry statement"
read to the media,
a day-old news bit
nearly as cold and dead as the
tragically hapless "hero" father,
who chose to fight an armed intruder
breaking into his home in broad daylight,
who chose to fight to protect his family
when there was no one there to protect him
from the police

What they mean

Out with perpetual friends
I now read a sharpness
in their eyes,
a hard squint that tells
their guards are up
against me,
me, their once entertaining joke man,
who loved
to tell amusing jokes
and funny, absurd stories

I hear a falsely casual line
floated for me to hear
on the far edge of sound,
he, meaning me,
should lighten up,
be his, meaning my, old fun self

They miss the old, laugh-hole un-bitter, me,
now so harsh with tense reality

Funny that-
almost a sarcastic joke in itself

What they mean
is they miss
the young me,

the apparently once easy-going,
lighthearted, fun guy
who used to
entertain his friends with
wit and frivolity

Eager for my entertainments,
they never imagined what it took
or how truly hard it is
to make others laugh

Like now, the constant pressure
to invent new jokes:
An interviewer asks "What do you, Bill Cosby
have to say about all the women
who accused you of rape?"
Old Bill doesn't skip a beat, he sez
with his comedic poker face
licking his purple lips in and out
like a fat old cunt
"Fuck'em if they can't take a joke."

See, that's what I mean

I'm not stupid or an amnesiac,
I miss the old me too,
each slipping away day
makes it tougher
for this heavy-heart to
make funny

I would like to resurrect him,
for these friends who are now
less funny themselves,
but,
what the hell
is so funny now?

Hell on earth

The plague of polio
is back
It's a killing disease
Prevention is
just a shot away
Act before it's too late

Children are stricken once again,
god damned unlucky victims-
if they survive-
ruined for life by parents
who failed to protect them
Think of it-
one shot away from preventable DEATH

Do you honestly need
the horror of the recent past
to teach you a lesson?

Get it this way-
"go viral" on social media
or read Wikipedia
about this highly contagious disease
with an updated, modern
March of Dimes freak out poster
displaying
the victim stripped bare
to expose the tragedy of post-polio "life,"
a degraded lifetime with useless apologies for

withered, decrepit, deformed,
uselessly paralyzed muscles and limbs
baring long jagged surgical scars,
a half-life barely preserved in iron lungs and
propped up by wheelchairs, walkers,
crutches, canes, heavy steel braces,
thick-soled orthopedic Frankenstein shoes
dragged by shortened, wasted legs

Stare hard at these "paltry things,"
past, aging survivors of this reborn terror,
doubly condemned by the evil "Post-Polio Syndrome,"
accelerating the wasting anew
Can you imagine?
A daily, incremental, uncontrollable loss of
already debilitated strength and energy, movement and independence,
re-occurring health afflictions
after all the painful surgeries to stem
polio's ravages

You, fearful parents,
worried by imaginary dire side-effects
of the vaccine,
how could you expect dumb luck or
meaningless prayers
to keep your children safe?
Polio vaccines
have saved millions of children
world-wide for sixty plus years,
forcing "the scourge" of polio to
the verge of extinction

In our shame and humiliation
we scream for your public attention
to our wasted bodies,
recoil in repulsion,
of what happened to innocent children
before Salk and Sabin invented
the vaccine
Act before it is too late

Our overcrowded planet,
with billions of potential victims,
why should anyone care who's afflicted as long
as it's somebody else's kid
somebody else's problem?
Let it happen anywhere else,
like a Third World Country
where witch doctor's still kill
health workers who volunteer
to inoculate and save their children
until the disease escapes and spreads
to your loved ones

Feel a terrified, helpless child
strapped down on a hospital gurney,
feel the stab of a spinal tap needle,
feel the forcefully thrust needle puncture
your spinal column,
feel the pressure of spinal fluid siphoned into a
syringe, feel the needle jerked back out
followed by an explosion of headaches
lasting for days

Better to strike yourself dead
than ever have to say, "I'm sorry,
I thought I was doing the right thing,"
confessing the hard, sad way
that disease and death
never sleep

Book sale at Fort Mason

Twice a year
six hundred feet
of book buyers
quietly line up
along the Fort Mason Pier,
brimming with hope
and empty book boxes that
anchor them like bollards in
the early morning fog,
anxious, yet patient and greedy
to begin another exciting
gold rush for
bargain priced used books
promptly at 4 p.m.

Hushed talk flows
through the fading gloom
dwarfed by the emerging
brick red skeleton
of the Golden Gate Bridge
and the cement grey loneliness
of Alcatraz escaping
from the fog

The two monuments like bookends
bracketing the pier

Bearing special opening night
admission tickets,

the huge crowd
of "Friends" of the Library
surge with door buster enthusiasm
into the gargantuan book sale
kindly set up by 2,000 volunteers

The Friends generously provide
shopping carts for use
like fishermen's nets for the ambitious
to haul in their precious books

A vision of book splendor appears
with vast numbers of tables
gorged with so many books that
many are left unpacked in boxes
beneath the tables

Buyer's carts soon bulge with books
voraciously culled
by the quick, the practiced,
the rapacious and the thorough

Late in the furious
book root-fest
the poetry tables, forever lacking
a single book by Charles Bukowski,
have been pillaged,
the left behind books splayed akimbo,
offering the rejected standard glut of anthologies,
self-published poetry books,
scorned book club editions,
a sprinkling of Ogden Nash

and several copies
of <u>This is my Beloved</u>

Then a joyous moment of serendipity-
there, astonishingly passed over,
lay a rare, beautiful copy
of the first edition, first state
in white covers of
<u>The Fall of America</u> by Allen Ginsberg
published by San Francisco's own
legendary City Lights bookstore
for a mere two bucks!

A splendid reward for a long days wait
begetting an instant happiness
of time well spent

Later you join
The Friends of the Library
who graciously host
a wine and cheese party,
reflecting upon the odds
that of the
random half million books
offered at this sale,
spread over 130,000 feet of warehouse space,
this perfect book was there for you

Allen Ginsberg satori

Sorry,
this is a long poem
I would have made shorter
if I could

It's about beat news,
a beat mystery
that means something
important
after all these years

A needy time
to divine a late satori

There could be only
ONE living person
who knew
the answer

My 20 year old theory,
a missing piece of
the beat source puzzle,
the vexing secret
still alive and hidden,
craving The CLIMAX,
like the incessant replay
of a dream lover
who works you up,

plays you all hot
and excited,
controlling the moment
just to say No,
no no, no no,
not yet,
so un-beat

To explain-
Once we hosted
Allen Ginsberg
for a private book signing
at Vagabond Books
The gracious legendary poet
arrived and we locked
ourselves in

Awestruck by Allen's presence-
so much living literary history-
we excitedly talked poetry and literature
and writing
as he signed a tall stack
of his handsome, important new book:
<u>Photographs</u>
drawing "AH" inside circles
he dated April 1, 1991

Allen asked us for a copy of
Wallace Stevens <u>Collected Poems</u>
which we luckily had
and gave to him
with pleasure and thanks

for coming to us,
for signing his books,
and for his help with the
balled-up literary estate of Jack Kerouac

Time and the river
flowed swift and calm
A couple photographs were taken
to record the precious moment

I spoke about Jack Kerouac,
eager to discover the origin
of his inspiration,
the "how"
of his radical transformation
from writing his first novel, The Town and The City,
in a Thomas Wolfe mode
to inventing the new, blazing, bebop,
"spontaneous style" of "automatic writing" for his
masterpiece On The Road

Where did this creative leap come from?

Besides Neal Cassady's once
long lost seminal beat letter,
what was the source of this literary trigger?
Like Walt Whitman's revolutionary poetic
break with the past,
what begat this new creation?

The passionate moment
to ask arrived

It went like this--
"Allen, I gotta ask you,"
"Mm, mmm, ok, sure."
"Thinking back a long time ago,
can you remember Jack Kerouac
reading Mezz Mezzrow's book
Really the Blues, before or while
Jack was writing On The Road?
I have to know,
because I think the Mezzrow book
was a key inspiration for Kerouac's
break-through writing form for "On the Road."

There it was,
my golden opportune still point,
burning so hot,
asked after years of
wonder

Allen fell pensive,
rolled his head to one side,
tilted his big head up,
sighed and gazed far back in time

He slowly lowered his eyes
and looked me
full in the face
and slowly began
nodding his head slowly,
like he was listening
to a silent raga
Allen answered quietly,

"Yes… yes, I remember…then… he did, we
did." Ah, there it was,
the connection, THE ANSWER!
The beat lover said yes,
oh excruciatingly sweet dreamed of yes! Yes! Yes!
A perfect climax!
Oh Allen,
bless you,
bless your memory!

Mezzrow collects Jack's dues
for <u>Really The Blues</u>

Blissful satori achieved,
this revelation
now shared with
you, patient readers

Yes, yes, yes,
ah yes, so John Lennon yes positive,
read it now,
think and reflect
upon this Kaddish,
joining the known history
of how it all began

L. A. riots

When you own
your own business
anything can happen
because it's mostly you
against the world

During the L A riots
we stayed open for
business
all the long riot days

There were no customers,
only the fools out
running the streets,
looting and shooting,
looking for opportunities
to steal anything,
free from police interference

We kept our door wide open
to make a point of our distain,
open, not exactly for business as usual,
but in defiance
of the scum running amok

We needed desperately,
like all working class bookstores
on the edge,

to make a few sales
to keep going,
to feed our family
and pay the rent

I kept a claw hammer
handy in my jacket pocket
in case I had to put up
a fight,
but the looters never bothered
our bookstore
To them,
plundering us wouldn't have been
much of a prize

The rioters and thieves
didn't scare me,
hard-up criminal opportunists mostly
who knew this was their only chance
for a big score,
being stupid, greedy assholes
with no regard for others

Looters charged
into the tailor's shop next door
and stole
a pile of discarded rags,
missing the repaired clothes
hanging behind the counter,
cheering loudly as they escaped
with their booty
raised high above their heads

showing off their treasure
to other rampaging thieves

Surreal memories persist
like when a looter
honked his horn
and waved his arm
madly out his window,
bouncing and scraping and weaving
down Westwood Boulevard
in his beat-up over loaded
pick-up truck
piled high with five stolen sofas,
the cushions falling out and
randomly bouncing
to lay scattered and abandoned
along the curbs

Women and men
"from the local community"
were caught on camera
for all to see
on the evening news,
escaping through the busted glass doors
of a Toy's R" Us store
on La Cienega,
arms loaded with
stolen toys

The miscreants torched buildings
all over L A and the stinking smoke
from burning stores

drifted as a pall over
the cities crime wave

Further south near the tracks below the 10 Freeway,
a lone, fire-gutted, roofless brick building
stood, still smoldering
with the words "BLACK OWNED" spray painted
in six foot letters
on the front,
while tagged on the side was another fresh
rage-painted sentiment, "FUCK THE PIGS!"

It was absurd and sickening
to watch this madness
of violence and murder,
our city ruled by anarchy,
day after day,
the night sky lit up by arson fires,
while our own anger grew
as the riots dragged on

In the fall
when our roof leaked,
I dug out a 38 caliber slug
from its deep hole
over our family room

Joe Herwig

I thought of
orphaned old books
with their musty perfume
smell slumbering on dusty and
dim old shelves
and Joe Herwig's bookstore
breezed into mind
from the far off,
mostly forgotten
good old times

Joe's store,
long gone,
Joe himself,
long dead

His slummy neighborhood,
his grand old spacious space
in San Diego
now lost to developers,
high marketing
to the tourist trade
as "The Gaslamp District,"
now smartly, successfully bursting
with vacationers
breathing reborn
fresh new air
while greedily sucking blood
from the Comic-Con

Humbug

Reading stale poetry
is like climbing
a ladder

Each shaky step summons up
the stock devices,
the–
if so's, what ifs,
thens and therefores,
and the slight-of-hand mumbo jumbo

Readers, listeners,
stupified by tedious stanzas
and artless blah, blah, blah,
phoney Greek reference this,
Roman arcane reference that,
maybe some Chinese junk thrown in like Pound did,
a snow job of the obscure
devoid of tonic novelty–
observe the verse reader stretch
one hand up, then
one foot up,
belaboring the dead ladder metaphor
ad nauseam–
a puerile image of fingers bumbling
like a keyboard monkey
slaying another simile–
the formula–

read, steal, write,
waiting out the accident
of dumb creation's restless palaver,
this befuddled dream of word
punching
haunted by the incessant, taunting echo-
"a writer writes."

The piqued humbug gazes down,
knowing his paltry books
never sell,
blaming his publisher
of course
Argh, deep down, hardly suffering for
"my art, my art"

Another blank verse moment-
the poetaster
measures his fall against
the slender attendance,
always a problem,
because this poetry cannot hold-

Tempted to leap
into the void of redundancy,
the word assassin cries out-
"Hey! Up here! Pay attention!
I've dropped my pants
for you"

Soon, if you stick around
to watch this tottering

thesaurus of ambition
launch his
comic fit of twaddle,
imagine the game
of Whack-A-Mole
assaulting the readers
who have learned to hate
poetry

Santa Cruz

How could you stoop
so low
as to beg for a job at
a rendering plant,
a vile, wretched rendering plant!

In Santa Cruz
you were dead broke and
homeless and couldn't risk a
vag charge, so you waited until
the park ranger
left Henry Cowell State Park
around 5 p.m.
allowing you to slip in
and skip paying the overnight fee
which you didn't have,
providing you could wake up
and escape by dawn,
waking stiff and cold in your sleeping bag
from lying on the hard bed
of your pick-up truck

The rendering plant was
my last hope for a shit job
I'd tried every employer
in the Yellow Pages
from Watsonville to Davenport

As a fresh, new college graduate,
after sacrificing so much
for so many years,
I couldn't imagine getting even a junk job
could be so tough

Right there,
squatting on the beautiful coast
north of town,
with strong ocean breezes
too weak
to blow the rotten stench
of death away,
these bastards made money
by crushing the corpses of dead animals

How degrading,
how utterly awful
to kill time at shift work,
squeezing the juice out of hapless animals
for your bread and butter,
just for a paycheck

In the reeking, putrid, airless building,
the smirking man in filthy stained overalls said,
"Sorry," not meaning it, "we're full up."

A half hour later
you sat feeling relieved and
not beaten, nor crushed,
not hopeless, nor defeated,

re-reading The Wasteland,
in need of a heady line,
a life preserver of words to sustain you
as you stared out from Light House Point,
until all the sunlight in the world
drowned in the fatal darkness of the empty sea

You overslept the next morning,
suddenly startled awake by police sirens
and ambulances
screaming up to
a campsite laid-out amidst ancient towering redwoods
less than 150 feet away

The park ranger didn't catch you leaving,
you were just another
invisible transient
scudding by

In town over coffee
the TV news reported
the night's tragedy-
four young boys had been axed to death
in their tent
at Henry Cowell State Park,
attacker and motive unknown,
a bloody continuation
of the inexplicable crime wave of
grizzly Santa Cruz murders

Why the slaughter
of these young boys?
Why not me?

I was just another bum
in the park
and nobody cared about bums

Who did it?
Why was the murderer
never caught?

By odd chance, twenty years later,
I was chatting with a customer
who let drop she was going back
to Santa Cruz
for a gathering of the families
of the slain boys

Instantly,
the shallow burial of that memory
shot through me

Because I couldn't help myself
I blurted out
that I had been there
that deadly night
A sudden awkward silence
like a guillotine
dropped between us,
then she hurriedly bought her books
and departed

I was glad I'd left Santa Cruz forever
Thinking back,
I saw I was wrong
For all the loser experiences

I'd had that pounded the hope
out of me,
by the slimmest chance
I wasn't the one
dead out of luck

Rain

The drought is on,
in full worry mode
with the city
and state
threatening stiff new penalties
for water wasters

Feeling creative today
because of a
sudden, ironic rain storm,
I wrote an essay
about our fun job of
finding vintage books
for the Madmen HBO show,
brewed another necessary pot
of coffee plus a latte
for my errant daughter, who
soon arrived breathless
and pleading for a special favor-
to park
her kooky pets
with us,
and to borrow our
gassed up car
to dash off
through the downpour,
all excited to celebrate
her joyous four day

bachelorette party
with her closest girlfriends
in Palm Springs

Later, I poured a glass
of red wine to continue
feeling the goodness
of this day,
enjoying the rare rain,
the rolling thunder
and the lightning storm
that refreshed Pasadena
all day

The rain
continues to drift down
through dark skies
while I am
stuck here
by the phone,
waiting for word
like always,
of her safe arrival

I refilled my
wine glass to
ease
my traditional
worry and impatience

It's been hours
since she left

Sheriff John

We never dreamed
Sheriff John wasn't
a real Sheriff

For nearly two decades
John Rovick starred in
Sheriff John's Lunch Brigade
sporting a warm, friendly, toothy smile
flashed between big ears
and a large heart you knew
was always there,
reaching out to you,
plus he wore a Sheriff's get-up
complete with an
official-looking
five-pointed star badge and
white cowboy hat

Sheriff John's hearty singing cheer brightened
our tiny Hoffman TV screen,
bringing comfort and delight to
homebound Brigadiers with the
cartoon adventures of
Crusader Rabbit
and his trusty side-kick
Rags the Tiger

Five days a week
Sheriff John sang
his catchy birthday song,
famously beginning
"Put another candle on my birthday cake,"
subtly reminding all viewers
about the passage of time-
"I'm another year old today"
Sheriff John then
read on air his birthday celebrants names

My Mom,
who treated perfect school attendance
as if it were the 11th Commandment,
kept me home only once
from elementary school,
on April 25th

To my 10 year old astonishment-
the great and wonderful Sheriff John
read my name off his
birthday wish list,
straight out to me and my mom,
then sang his birthday song
to us
This childhood moment
remembered with warm memories
every birthday since

Sheriff John Rovick's surprise newspaper
obituary,
offered, besides the shock,
a piece of his personal history

to his Brigade of aging adults
that never knew
about the 50 combat missions
he flew in a B-25 during
World War 2

A quiet war hero
who lived and fought bravely
and survived the evils
of history
and chose in civilian life
to spread cheer and happiness
to the first generation
of post war baby boomer TV kids,
invoking goodness in youngsters
by wise example
and who merrily sang
"Laugh and be happy
and the world will laugh with you."
RIP

Walking on tacks

There's another self-serving
neuropathy ad
in the newspaper
picturing a foot poised
to step on thumb tacks

I've done that-
stepped on a real
tack and it hurt like
hell,
instantly jabbing a sleepy 3 a.m. brain
from borderline consciousness to
cruelly invoking my grumpy emergency ontology
with disbelief,
"no, no, no, not possible, not happening"
But it did

This accident in the numbed darkness
is no fictional ad, fuck no,
registering a stupid personal misery,
alone,
unbalanced on one oldster foot,
unable to reach the embedded tack
and pry it out,
or hop, rictus bound,
to the safety of a nearby chair

Such an ordinary movement,
suddenly stymied

after the habit of walking in darkness
an entire lifetime,
again, not possible,
doubt still alive
in your gimpy heart
But there it was

Fear drives so much
of precarious life

This ad, out to scare
a few more bucks
from the gullible
by conniving capitalists
who would have you hung
upside down by your heels
to profit from your pain
if you let them,
and in return,
if you were a vindictive victim,
you could wish them your disease

What it's like,
is every living second of your remaining life,
a Sisyphean prisoner in a pit
of electric eels,
enduring their powerful movements
beneath your squishy soles,
slithering up around your ankles while
burning the bottoms of your feet,
searing you
with their relentless bolts of fire

Goddamn, there is no cure-
these huckster placebos
are for suckers

Sleep on, sleep on sleeping pills, a
half-life in brain dead darkness so
far from the light,
no ads can abate your dreams
or wake you from this
false and costly panacea during
the wash of your stinging,
waking hours

Can you feel what I am saying?
What is most real
is the pain
these afflicted,
aging victims
with their used up bodies
can't escape

It's like dying from the feet up

Imagine yourself

Imagine yourself
ashes in an urn,
imagine yourself
pickled and bloodless
lying in a strong box
of oblivion,
buried under a ton
of heartless earth,
forever crushing
your escape

Imagine yourself locked
in silent darkness, while
on weekends
visitors come to provoke memories
and pay respects,
while children trailing toys
frolic, ignorant
of the horror trapped beneath
their gamboling feet

Imagine a dog's tail whipping
with frenzied excitement
your urn off a coffee table,
ignobly tumbling you out
from your memorial holding pen,
your grey ashes powdering across the floor
like stale flour,

to mingle until swept up
from this accidental awkward moment
leavened with dust bunnies

Imagine your future wilco,
the end after the end,
without a wince
if you
can

Class warfare

Most of us
don't start out
with much

Most of us
can't do much
about it

Along the way,
granted the freedom
to starve,
most of us do
what we can,
unwillingly circumscribed
at birth

There are moments
in every life
that make you sick,
when the stinginess
of humanity
would kick you out
further than the farthest star
and leave you there,
secretly cheering
your disappearance

The poorest education
cannot fail to teach you
the lesson of your
inconsequential life,
because we aren't
"created equal,"
no, with jealousy
and resentment we
are barely even
created at all

And when you rise up
from your exile and estrangement,
enraged and possessed
by your righteous struggle,
fight for yourself
with what you have
against the clubby league of undertakers,
these greedy strangers
ready to
bury you

Vals

The stigma was real
because it was meant
for you
Every surf day
you were judged
as an outsider
by the spoiled gang
of local Malibu and Palos Verdes assholes
that plied the same waves,
acting like
they owned the public beach
and you were a foreign invader,
another wetback
whose presence meant
you were there
to squeeze them out

Your surf skills offended them
by riding the hottest waves,
ignoring the wave pigs and wave bullies
determined to steal your right to ride
like everybody else

On benches, on sidewalks,
on the Malibu wall itself
local prick graffiti tags
threatened-
VALLEY GO HOME

and
NO VALS
and FTV
meant to intimidate outsider surfers
from entering their false domain-
often flattening your tires,
smashing your car windows,
and stealing your stuff
off the beach

Anger made you wish
great white sharks
would attack
and rip these selfish creeps
to shreds,
allowing you to
surf the red waves
in peace

If you allowed them
to rule the waves
like a despotic fiefdom
they'd have had your
head on a pike

If you'd let them,
these spoiled scions
would have poured
broken glass atop every wave
to keep you out,
like living close to the beach
gave them special privileges

just because they were lucky
to live nearby
and you weren't

October 31st

The milk thistle
has failed to slow
this chronic galloping chocolate cirrhosis

Halloween night
you sit by the front door
wearing a fool's cap and a Batman T-shirt,
a tumbler of
gassy tonic water
in hand,
your nod to the ghost
of parties past

Knock, knock,
the trick or treaters
bounce up the steps fast
and thick to breach my
welcoming doorway,
costumed, breathless and sparkle eyed,
jacked up on sugar rushes
in mad flight about the neighborhood,
block after block

Where are all these kids
the rest of the year?

How odd
tonight is special enough
to mitigate some hard parent rules

like, "never talk to strangers"
and "never take candy from strangers"
thus teaching kids a lesson in
adult ambiguity and the seminal idea
of applied relativity,
imploring some to wonder
what does "never" mean?

OK for now,
parent's hang back
in the darkness,
nervously positing their children
and adult fears
on stranger's porches,
trailing other kids
and memories

Young timid kids, wary and frightened
by the fake spider webs, hanging sheet ghosts,
cardboard gravestones, plastic skulls,
and flaming pumpkins
approach sheepishly alongside
aggressively scary costumed kids
with their outstretched swag bags,
some thanking you with relief
to make another safe getaway,
thinking, like you did as a kid,
how crazy fun and out of joint
this night is

The last vampire
collects my final candy handout
around 10,

like me once,
so eager this night
should last forever

In the bright morning sunlight
twisted and ripped candy wrappers
of Almond Joy, and Milky Way,
Snickers, Butterfingers and M & M's
decorate the sidewalks
like a candy hangover

Down

We are down to
one cat now

Sweet, loyal, old Ricky
hugged his food dish
for the last time
and at age 19
went to sleep forever

Like Ferdinand the Bull
I buried Ricky
beneath his favorite
shade tree,
which was laden with
ripe oranges

Maggie, age 3,
our last cat,
loves
us like an only
child

When I pet her
she purrs,
and raises her chin
with a dreamy smile

I expect she will
outlast us,
and am sorry to think
of her
as an orphan

For better or for worse

Sometimes we're good,
mostly good,
except when you
demand to bully talk
the night to death
and yell at me "fuck you!"
just in case I
have something to say

I agree
with you silently,
falling into sickened little pieces,
Fuck me!
Fuck me!
Fuck me!
You are so right

Milk

The tireless Ed Ruscha
City/Ruby poster from 1971
leans against the fireplace wall,
patiently resigned to never hang

The cat lies ball-tucked
upon her portly pillow

A glass of milk
half-glows beneath the reading lamp
whose base is surrounded
by family photos guarding this moment

Nearly midnight,
at rest,
all quiet,
a Happy Valentine's Day

In two

parts,

each body

is divided

One arm is

stronger,

more skillful

than the other,

one eye always

born to lead,

random skin blemishes

visibly less prominent

on the good side,

one ball

looms larger, lower,

one breast distends fuller,

one leg flexes

with keener balance

and power,

a cleaving

of paired

doubles,

alas,

even in youthful beauty,

asymmetrical

A rotting cantaloupe

lay unharvested

in a dry field

When the cantaloupe

broke open

it was filled with

white wiggly maggots

and the maggots

quickly grew into white people

who planted more

cantaloupes

that rotted and

turned black and

imploded

only to

burst forth with

more maggots

who turned into

more people

until the whole world

grew spoiled and

caved in from so

many maggots

and everyone

and everything died

including the maggots,

especially the maggots

and then the earth

was finally

peaceful and silent

again

A note to the reader—

False Positive is the 13th book published by VagabondBooks in celebration of our 44th year of bookselling.

Author's previous books

BOOK HOLOCAUST
LITTLE WHITE SAMBO
PHANTOM PAIN

Made in the USA
Columbia, SC
11 November 2017